J HERRERA

What Happens in Vegas, Family Edition

Find out there's more to Vegas than what meets the Adult eye

This book was professionally typeset on Reedsy.
Find out more at reedsy.com

This book is Dedicated to my Husband, I Love you Forever. Thank you for always supporting me in every and all crazy endeavors. You inspire me, watching you get up at the crack of dawn everyday knowing you probably won't get home till the sun goes down, walking into the house looking like a Concrete Raccoon, All to support our Family. I am truly grateful for you. To the Families who we had the pleasure of sharing these beautiful Las Vegas Memories with, can't wait to make more!

Lost Time is Never Found Again...

-Benjamin Franklin

Contents

1

Introduction

They say "What happens in Vegas, Stays in Vegas." Well, that's not the case here. This is the Family Edition Vegas Vacation, and you and I both know whatever happens in Vegas, those kids are going home and Telling Everyone! So let's make sure we make GREAT memories and that not all of the things the kids repeat will be embarrassing truths about Mom and Dad. We unfortunately do not have any control over all the other stuff they might see in the wild nightlife of Vegas. They might see the dressed in white Bride and her Bachelorette group of girls with white and pink feather boas, drinking out of genitalia looking straws dancing their lives away to elevator music. They might even catch the not so rare sighting of Captain Courageous and his crew of men, Newly single ready to mingle! They're there to help their low key devastated brother get over his cheating ex-girlfriend. We call those the "FREE SHOWS" it's all in FUN and Vegas Baby!

So, a little information on me... I'm happily married to my favorite person, my Partner in crime. We have 4 kids! Yea I know, no T.V and all that good stuff that happens when two people are in love and so the beat goes on. Long story short, we started with 1 baby which quickly

1

turned into 2 babies in the first twelve months. Irish twins are what they're called, one mother having two children who are born 12 months or less apart. Seven beautiful years after that we got lucky IN VEGAS and landed that Two for One deal. REAL LIFE TWINS, two handsome Baby Boys. That is proof for you, that "What happens in Vegas, does not stay in Vegas" they show up nine months later. Now, here I am sharing my Mommy Vegas vacation secrets with you, so let's get to it!

This book is yours to keep, put your brain on pilot mode and let me guide you through Vegas because having to watch over your kids and enjoy yourself at the same time is already a hard enough job in itself. First rule, there are NO RULES! Hello, we're in Vegas! Flip to whichever chapter you see fit for the moment you are living right now. If you're over the strip and need to take a breath of Fresh Air, skip over to the nature chapter to find out what awesome stuff there is to do outdoors. Enjoy what Mother Nature has to offer and what beautiful secrets she has hidden in Vegas so well, that all the people who are too drunk will NEVER FIND IT! Yay! I'm kidding, ish.

If you're a Planner, kudos to you. You have already hit the JackPot on this Book and you haven't even gotten to Vegas yet! HIGH FIVE! I'm here to help, I'll tell you what to pack and what not to forget to pack. What places are a "MUST STOP" if you're driving the fam to vegas, you'll probably have to make potty stops every 30 minutes anyways. I also have some fun history about Vegas to help the drive go by a little faster, or maybe you're chillin poolside while the kids splash around and enjoy the millions of awesome pools found in every hotel. Kids are hungry, where do we take them? Hurry, open up the chapter on kid friendly places to grub. Whatever your deal is, I got your back!

So, without future adieu, LET'S DO THIS!

2

"Las Vegas, A Gangster's Paradise!" The History behind Sin City

The Valley was first inhabited by nomadic Paleo-Indians, then came the Anasazi, who were smart enough to leave proof, "Anasazi People were HERE!" 2,100 year old Historian petroglyphs found in the Valley of the fire state Park is proof of that. All of a sudden POOF GONE, I guess. supposedly these people just vanished! The Paitute people quietly and peacefully settled in here as well after that.

Fast Forward to the 19th Century and Along came this European Fellow in 1829 named Rafael Riviera, who arrived in the valley on accidental purpose. That's right, he was bored of the same ol route from Sante Fe to Los Angeles and decided to try something new and different, 100 miles difference to be exact. The original route was founded by Mexican explorer Antonio Armijo, making his way from New Mexico to California, he named this route The Old Spanish Trail. So, we can just assume that's why Rafael decided to try something NEW, because the Spanish Trail was well, OLD. Never be afraid to try something new, thanks to that decision, Mr. Riviera was rewarded abundantly and overflowing. A literal Oasis of Las Vegas Springs, he happily named his newly found miracle "Las Vegas" which is Spanish meaning "The Meadows."

Believe it or not, the Church was next up on the Guest List. 1858, when the Mormons came to town and settled in the half-way mark between Salt Lake City and Los Angeles to keep a close eye on their newly made mail route. They built Forts, planted crops, and made jobs for themselves mining for lead. Then one day after many failed crop attempts, they decided "Eff this, It's too HOT, We're out!" didn't even pick up and leave, they just straight bounced. Abandoned Forts can still be seen at the crossings of Las Vegas Blvd and Washington Ave.

Shout out to the Union Pacific Railroad project and William A. Clark for putting Las Vegas on the Map, May 15, 1905. (Again, trying something new is always a good idea) He saw the potential in Vegas and took a chance, made the purchase, and got right to business securing water rights to the spring, hired some dudes and built the railroad track featured in the image above that would soon be the main connection between Salt Lake City and Los Angeles. Persistent in his efforts, Clark didn't stop there, he turned a Major profit by selling off over 600 lots in one day including Vegas' first unofficial non operating Casino,"Station Cafe," creating a whole New Town around his Locomotive Stop.

The Wild Wild West was then born. A city filled with mostly Cowboys and Railroad workers with simply too much money then they knew what to do with. What happens when people have too much money and not much sense about what to do with it? WE BLOW IT, Proof that "blowing money in Vegas" goes all the way back in time! In 1906 The Golden Gate Casino (org named Hotel Nevada) opened up as the first and long-term casino, located on Fremont Street. Birthing a luscious red light district filled with speakeasies and many bootleg casinos paying no mind to the 1910 Ban on Gambling, the wild wild west grew up to become SIN CITY. Hence "SIN" City, due to no one giving a crap about laws!

Thanks to the once again legalization of gambling, and the 1931 construction of the Hoover Dam, there was a monumental turning point for the city of Las Vegas. It not only secured the source of water but also the inflow of people. Not too long after that, Sin City caught the eye of another man who saw much potential in this lavish city, Legendary East Coast Mobster Bugsy Siegel. Who brought on his business partner, Mob Boss Meyer Lanskey aka the "Bugs and Meyers Mob," they quickly planted roots here in Sin City. It was then that organized crime was introduced. Vegas opened its doors to the very first Luxurious Hotel Resort here on the Strip, The Flamingo Resort in 1946. Although short lived, it was fun while it lasted for Ol'Bugsy, he was murdered in 1947, only six months after his opening. Thanks to Bugsy and his team, The Flamingo set a new standard in Vegas. Shortly after more and more Luxury Hotels began popping up on the strip. Business was BOOMING, so much so that even Sinatra, and Elvis showed up, and might I add, SHOWED OUT! Man, I wish I had a time machine sometimes, those are performances you definitely wouldn't want to miss.

In 1966, billionaire businessman Howard Hughes showed up and decided it was "Time To Clean House!" He made it a point to slowly buy out as many Mob owned hotels as he could. Financially owned and run Mafia Hotels were a thing of the past by 1980.

Inspiration struck, for the rebirth of Las Vegas, more and more Hotels, Motels, Restaurants, and Venues arose to be what we now know as a cleaner, less deadlier version of LAS VEGAS! It is still known today as the Entertainment Capital of the World.

So what are you waiting for? GO BE ENTERTAINED!!

3

"Goodbye Reality, HELLO VEGAS!" Don't Forget Your Kids

Make your PACKING LIST

F irst check the weather, we usually go Late Winter-spring or Late Summer-Fall. Remember, always try to pack lightly. You are not MOVING to Vegas, it's just a few days, maybe a Weekend trip.

Let's start with our suites, from the bottom up.

Mom

1. Shoes/Sandals (My go to pairs are Tevas, ready for anything & cute)
2. Socks
3. Underwear
4. Nightdress
5. Swimsuit
6. Swimsuit cover

7. 2 Shorts, 1 athletic
8. 2 Pants, 1 sweatpant
9. Shirts/Blouses
10. Jacket (Light,if for summer/fall)
11. Bras, 1 Sport
12. Sun hat, baseball cap, hair scrunchies
13. Light Jewelry
14. Purse/wallet

Dad

1. Everyday Shoes for walking & Hiking
2. Sandals
3. Socks
4. Underwear
5. Basketball shorts
6. Swim Shorts
7. Shorts, shorts
8. 2 Pants, 1 sweatpant
9. T-shirts/Tanks
10. Jacket (Light,if for summer/fall)
11. Shades
12. Wallet

Kids

1. Everyday Shoes for walking & Hiking
2. Sandals
3. Socks

4. Underwear
5. Jammies
6. Shorts
7. 2 Pants, 1 sweatpant
8. Swimsuit
9. Arm Floaties
10. Goggles
11. T-shirts/Tanks
12. Jacket (Light,if for summer/fall)
13. Hat to block the sun, bucket or baseball

Toiletries

1. Shamp/Cond (I'm picky)
2. Leave-in Conditioner for Mom & Sissy
3. Gel for Dad & the Boys
4. Brush & Comb
5. Toothpaste
6. Toothbrushes
7. Floss
8. Facewash, Face Lotion, Toner
9. Body Lotion travel size
10. Body soap (again, picky)
11. Menstrual products, if it's about that time
12. Make up
13. Sunscreen

Extras

1. Phone
2. ipad/tablet
3. CHARGERS
4. Card Games for kids
5. Activity/Coloring Book & Crayons
6. A Book, Specifically this one and 1 other/per child
7. Firestick & Remote
8. Envelope of Play Monies for Mommy & Daddy

Where to stay & When to go

There are so many Hotels to choose from, I know it can feel overwhelming trying to find the perfect place for you and your family to rest your heads. I'm going to break it down from the Least expensive, to the Most expensive. Keep in mind it also matters what day of the week you first arrive. The Best times of the month to go are Jan-April, DO NOT even attempt Spring Break, everyone and their Mama wants to be there during this "Peak Weather time" Rates are at their highest. Sep-Nov right before that Christmas Holiday wave. You can also sometimes score in July and August, being as those are the HOTTEST times to be in Vegas. Make sure you're ready to endure this type of heat though. The heat index for Vegas Summers is somewhere between OMG and WTF!

Mommy Tip: Arrive Sunday, stay till Wednesday. It's not only cheaper, but WAY less crazy and cleaner. For your last minute Hotel bookings, Check out Hotels Tonight if you have not already to find the best rates. Downside; their cancellation policy is not too hot, so just make sure you're serious about this trip. When using Hotels Tonight make sure it's after 4pm, and you're searching in "Incognito" mode for less price inflation. Every Hotel with availability wants to book out, so they will give you the "HOT DEAL" for a great bargain. Mess around and land that G Suit for what you would have paid for a weekend stay!

Now that you're all OFFICIALLY HERE! YAY! Let's talk about where to stay. I've tried my best to list these Hotels in order of least expensive to most expensive.

HOTELS & RESORTS

Circus Circus, Just driving up to this HUMONGOUS circus themed Hotel will have the kids all riled up and ready for a fun vacation. This place has been a well known family favorite since 1968 for its inexpensive rates and of course, THE CIRCUS. It's not the most luxurious place to stay, but from a kid's pov, THIS IS IT, game over THEY WIN! You'll be staying above the largest Arcade/Theme Park in Las Vegas. The Party is literally right beneath your feet. Be prepared for a FULL day of "The Adventuredome '', and yes, I am Totally Serious; it takes a whole day to get through this theme park. The Pool area is also like a mini water theme park. I guess the only downside to this hotel is that it's far from the strip; like get in your car and drive there kinda far! ❧

Rates: Low $26 - Peak $222 per/night

Excalibur, Our family FAVORITE so far. My kids literally go bonkers when they see the Castle! I personally love it here, because #1 The Fun Dungeon; this arcade is big enough to enjoy a night of video games and prizes, but not big enough to break the bank over one night. #2 The Tournament of Kings, who wouldn't want to pretend they are back in Medieval times? Secretly watch the kids' excitement as they clap and Cheer their favorite Knights on like no one is watching. #3 They have not two, but FOUR pools to choose from!? I promise it takes a few return visits before your kids ask to try out another Hotel Pool (1 Adult only pool). #4 The rates are great, we're able to stay in a comfy hotel and have a comfy amount of playing money left in the budget so we can do what we came here to do, HAVE FUN! ❀

Rates: Low $29 – Peak $284 per/night

Bally's is centered in the heart of Las Vegas, giving this hotel an awesome view from the Jubilee Tower. Tip: Opt for the North side of the Tower for a great view of the Baellagio's Fountain Show. The younger kids never get tired of watching that water shoot up and down, over and over. Ah, to be a kid again... Speaking of, Bally's Blu Pool area has a giant pool and is equipped with an outdoor playing area the kids will enjoy. Unfortunately No indoor Arcade, sorry I had to give it to you straight, BUT you are close enough to bounce around and still have fun at neighbor arcades. As a guest of Bally's you can visit 3 different pools pro bono, these include Planet Hollywood, Paris, and Flamingo. *⁜

Rates: Low $31 - Peak $ 247 per/night

New York New York, This moderately priced hotel is known for their NYC themed rooms, and roller coaster, The Big Apple Coaster. If you have a Thrill Seeker in the family, I suggest you "Let'em Ride!" I know my older kids had a blast on it. They also have a decent sized Arcade that the kids will love. The variety in affordable restaurants will NOT disappoint your picky eaters. New York New York is also not too far a walking distance from The Park, located between the hotel and Park MGM, one of the sightseeing adventures I mention later. 🐾

  Rates: Low $44 – Peak $360 per/night

Flamingo, Being the Oldest hotel on the strip; The Flamingo has been around since 1946! Standing out in their pink modern, updated rooms, you would never know. Like Bally's this hotel is also centrally located, giving it the best views in town at an adorable rate. Your kids will LOVE the pool area, not only do you feel like you're in the Tropics somewhere with all the beautiful greenery. But the pool is pretty much a meeting point between a Lagoon, a Waterfall, and a Water Slide! Say what?! I know that's awesome, right? It does not stop there, this Resort also has a Wildlife Habitat where you and the fam can check out the Flamingo's who live there and a few of their bird buddies. 🐾

Rates: Low $27 - Peak $364 per/night

The Cancun Resort, For an OFF the Strip experience which some parents love, The Cancun Resort is a great option. They offer a little more kid friendly activities and parent loving amenities. To help keep the cost of eating out under control, sometimes it is advisable to opt for the hotel with the kitchenette. This also helps keep the home routine going for the easily thrown off younger kids. The fam will have options, and that's a GREAT thing, right? Cancun Resort owns up to their name with their pool area. Other activities include a Game room equipped with pool tables, foosball, and table tennis.

Rates: Low $79 – Peak $380 per/night

Photo by George Landis

Mandalay Bay, This Heavy Hitter, comes in at 7th place for us due to its higher rates. If you have the money to splurge, DO IT! It's a One Stop Shop, you could literally just stay here and not even have to leave the whole time you're on vacation. This Resort offers a huge array of food options at all different price points for every meal time. There is so much to explore here, you WILL get lost. I'm totally serious, so please don't let your kids run around unsupervised, ya know Mom to Mom, I don't want your heart to skip any beats. DO NOT forget your Ice Chest as they do not provide a mini fridge, even though this hotel is so expensive. Your kids will be so excited to visit the Shark Reef Aquarium, they will lose their $#%@! When they find out they can Actually feed A Shark! BOOM, Done! You've just won the Kids choice Award for BEST PARENTS EVER just for choosing to stay in this Resort. Congratulations! ❀

Rates: Low $79 - High $444 per/night

Road Trip

Most Families who visit Vegas are pretty local, at least enough to all squeeze into your Soccer Mom VAN and arrive at your destination in style! Hit all 13 Lucky stops and you might just "WIN IT BIG" when you arrive!

Lucky 13 Stops from Los Angeles to Las Vegas

1. Mormon Rocks
2. Bottletree Ranch

3. California Route 66 Museum
4. Barstow Historic McDonald Train Station
5. Calico Ghost Town
6. EddieWorld
7. Liberty Sculpture Park
8. Peggy Sue's Diner
9. Alien Jerky
10. Baker World's Largest Thermometer
11. Valley Wells Rest Stop for the quick History Lesson
12. Bonnie & Clyde Exhibition inside Whiskey Petes
13. Outdoor World Bass Pro Shops

4

"Go Big or GO HOME!" Family Attractions & Entertainment

A ll Entertainment and Attractions listed below are for any and all aged kids, I really didn't want to get too age specific or this book would be never ending. Use your best judgment, no one knows your kids better than you and you don't need a book to tell you that. These are in no specific order. For current pricing, visitor tips and all that good stuff please make sure you visit their websites before showing up, that way there are no surprises and if there's a deal on tickets you can score those too.

FAMILY PHOTO CHALLENGE
Pictures are FOREVER, Please don't forget to capture the moment with your Family while visiting. Yes, live in the moment as well, but moments can be forgotten.

ATTRACTIONS

Shark Reef Aquarium

The Aquarium inside Mandalay Bay is just SO awesome, something about an aquarium just brings peace to mind. They also have an Undersea Explorers VR Experience, which is pretty cool. The kids will love the hands on activities, you can pet a Stingray and a Starfish! There is plenty more to explore but make sure you check out the shipwreck tank as shown in the picture above, as my Family loved that experience.

Neon Museum and Boneyard

I admit it, Fine! Yes, I made us splurge on this one. Mom is a HUGE fan of art, and a history junky. So of course, we HAD to visit! My kids ended up having a good time too, admittedly not as good a time as I did tho. They're awesome pieces of art no doubt, but unless you have some knowledge and appreciation of "what used to be old town Vegas" it just doesn't hit at the same level of excitement. Do your homework before you go, so you can enjoy the full effect of nostalgia and surrealness of these iconic signs. Man how I wish I could have seen them all LIT UP in all their beauty, shining down on the streets of The Original Glitter Gulch. All and all this place is a MUST, no matter what, it's totally awesome.

Siegfried and Roy's Secret Garden and Dolphin Habitat

OK, WHOA! Who knew there are actual Tigers, Lions, and Dolphins ON the strip. Look no further if you have zero plans of driving off the strip and you feel like the family needs some time outdoors, this Secret Garden does not disappoint. Actually, they've managed to input so much greenery in this habitat that you forget where you are. Siegfried and Roy strive to give these endangered animals the life and home they deserve. Awe, that's amazingly beautiful.

VEGAS SHOWS

Photo by George Landis

Mystere Cirque du Soleil

This is a 90 minute show, for any age really. Kids and parents alike can all get lost in the weirdness of this show, acrobatics, dancers and colors of the show will not allow you to look away.

Photo by George Landis

Tournament of Kings

This is a 90 minute show. Our family Fave, like I said before; all the action, horses and excitement is just so much fun for the family, I know yours will enjoy it as well. This show is filled with horse racing, jousting, and sword fighting. It is a meal and show bundle, but remember you're more so there for the show. The food is a little bland if i'm being honest, but then again, what more could you expect from food that is supposed to have been from the Medieval period.

Blue Man Group

At 105 minutes this show is a bit lengthier but well worth it, it's so entertaining you won't even notice the time. The Blue Man Group is pretty much a Rock Concert/Comedy show. It will get pretty loud, and the whole family will be pumped!

Photo by George Landis

The Beatles LOVE

A 90 minute show. This is hands down MY fave, I just loved ALL of it. The show took us all the way back to the 60's on a TRIP through Strawberry Fields. The music was duh, AMAZING, its The Beatles. There are aerial stunts, acrobats, BUBBLES, what kid doesn't LOVE bubbles? All and all this show is an all time Fan Fave by all. As a huge Beatles fan, it's just wrong if you don't attend at least once. You'll be back for more, they always do. "There's nowhere you can be that isn't where you're meant to be." -The Beatles

Gregory Popovch's Comedy Pet Theater

A 60 minute show. If you're a Family of Pet lovers, this show is for you! This Comedy show is mixed in with Circus acts as well. The family will be laughing and engaged in all the fun going on.

Terry Fator: Who's the Dummy Now

A 70 minute show. This Guy is Great, he has some mad skills with those puppets. Not only can he sing without moving his lips, I know, crazy right? He also managed to give all his Puppet colleagues their own personalities, they're all so funny! The family won't be able to stop laughing.

Thrill Seekers ONLY

Adventuredome Theme Park

Family Favorite, for sure. This is definitely an ALL day event, expect to drag your children kicking and screaming out of this place! It's that much fun, there are well over 25 rides. The food, like any other Theme park is a little overpriced and well, Theme Park food. Still yummy and affordable enough to keep the fun going! Cost: $$

Sky Jump at the STRAT

Bungy Jump off the Strat Hotel. For MAJOR Dare Devil's, Not me or any of mine. Thanks but no thanks. If you want your heart to fall out of your butt, this is for YOU! Cost: $$$

Insanity ride also at the STRATOSPHERE HOTEL

900 ft in the air, hanging off the side of the Strat while being spun around. Don't worry you are securely harnessed in this ride, and you probably won't even remember it, due to passing out from fear. It'll be over before you know it, have Fun! Cost:$$

High Roller at the LINQ

Scan the web to find a deal for this baby, because your family will definitely want to get on this HUGE Ferris Wheel. It's a great time as the Family is all huddled up into one little dome as you round about into the air overlooking the whole Las Vegas Strip. "Hey, I can see my house from here!" Cost:$$$

FlyLINQ Zipline at the Linq

Get into your Superman Flying Positions and get ready to Zipline over the famous LINQ Promenade. Try to fight the urge of closing your eyes because you literally ZIP right over! Cost: $$

Big Apple Coaster New York New York

Stick out that thumb and flag yourself down one of these Taxi Cabs because this ride is actually Super Fun! The older kids dig it, while the younger kids cry because they're too short to ride. It's ok, keep the little ones occupied in the arcade directly beside the entrance to this Coaster. Cost:$$

Arcade Fun

Circus Circus' Carnival Midway

Like mentioned before, this theme park has hours, hours, and hours of fun to be had here. With mini arcades stationed all around this facility even the parents won't be bored; take that dang Arcade Playing card and have at it while your kids wait in line for their next ride. Somewhere in that Labrinth of Arcade games you will find an area strictly filled with "The Classics." These are Parent Favorites as it takes us back to the Good Ol Days! The fun Does Not even stop there, Don't leave without visiting the actual Carnival. There is an area dedicated to Carnival Themed games only, remember the games that came to town set up then after a weekend left? Well, not this Carnival, it's HERE ALL YEAR LONG! Oh yea!

New York New York's The Big Apple Coaster & Arcade

The thing I love about this Arcade is the size of it. You can genuinely argue with your kids that you have taken them to the arcade and "Sorry it's over so soon but you've played all the games already, Let's go on to the next attraction." Small enough not to get stuck there for hours, Big enough to have some fun, Yup, I LIKE IT!

Excalibur's Fun Dungeon

Size wise, this Arcade falls in between Carnival Midway and The Big Apple Arcade. It's filled with plenty of games to have a great time and well worth the stop. It will take you about 60-90 minutes to get through this arcade. Thankfully it is conveniently placed right by the exit leading to Excalibur's North tram station, Connecting you to your next destination. New York New York's Big Apple Coaster & Arcade. Not in the mood for another Arcade? Tell the kids it's "Closed today!" Ssshh, we won't tell anyone you lied; afterall, We are in Sin City!

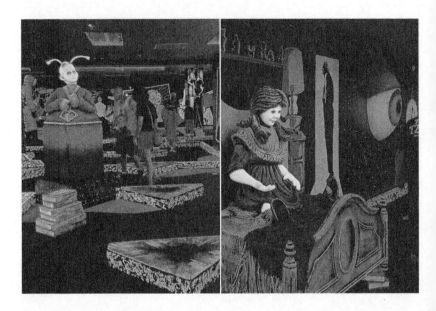

Twilight Zone Blacklight Mini Golf

Mini Golfing is fun already, add a blacklight and some trippy Twilight setups and this Family is SOLD! Our Family chose to celebrate a Birthday here. It was a great time hanging out watching no one get a hole in one and learning patience while the younger kids putt 50+ times to get that ball in the hole. Thank God there was so much cool stuff to stare at, you gotta love those Toddlers they're just so dang cute.

Fun Stop Shops, Kid Edition

Vegas is not only known for their extravagant, eye popping, show stopping Entertainment but also for their love of Retail Therapy. You can shop your way around the World here in Las Vegas. There are well over 250 shops that we WILL NOT be visiting. Sorry, but I think you forgot, We're here with The Fam! No worries, I'm here to help you choose those battles wisely. Kids hate shopping just as much as Parents hate shopping with kids. So let's just stick to the shops we can enjoy TOGETHER, Sugar anyone? It's pretty obvious the only things kids like to shop for are Candy, and Toys! This Mom doesn't shop, but no worries, we still got you covered. We'll be following my God Daughter and her family around as they seem to have gotten the Kids Version of shopping in Vegas down pact!

The LINQ Promenade

First up, LINQ promenade which includes a variety of yummy shopping. **I LOVE SUGAR** is located here, two stories of all things candy. They also have Sprinkles cupcakes, Ghirardelli, and Honolulu Cookie co. On the non perishable side; stores to visit here would be, Welcome to Las Vegas gift shop, Harley Davidson, Socks & Bottoms, and don't forget to grab your kids some nice bath time goodies for later at Nectar Bath Treats. Hopefully your family booked one of the many resort suits here in Vegas that include the biggest bathtubs you have ever seen.

HERSHEY'S Chocolate World

Take Full advantage of all the photo opportunities Hershley's Chocolate World has to offer. They have two stories of any candy ever made by this company and plenty of merch along with the sweets. Don't forget to stop by to see Vegas' very own TWIZZLER Lady of Liberty. The Bakery shop is a MUST, they offer all kinds of delicious treats and drinks. There is something for every family member, from S'mores, Milk shakes, baked goods, and coffee, they even have Chocolate BEER. Yes folks, they have literally thought of everything!

HELLO KITTY CAFE

Hello Kitty is so awesome she has two stores in Vegas. There is one located in The Fashion Show, and this one featured here is at Park MGM. The sweet treats offered here are almost too cute to eat! But don't waste food, you know starving kids and all, PLUS it's Delicious!

M&M's World

This M&M World is the first of its kind and is four stories tall. You can lose your child here, so hold onto them! The whole family will be blown away with all things M&M here. You won't even have time to snap a photo of them, which is ok because chances are, they're not even looking into the camera because "Whoa, Look over there!"

Coca-Cola Store

If you're anything like me, right about now you're Going Down, about two minutes away from face planting into that yucky strip floor. Hurry, this is a caffeine emergency. Pop in next door for that well deserved, satisfying, caffeinated Sodie Pop and history lesson on all things Coca-Cola.

5

"Keep Calm and Go to Vegas" Family Fun on a Budget

B ellagio Conservatory & Botanical Gardens
As you can see, This Garden is "Kind of a BIG DEAL." We've returned to this amazing Botanical Beauty time and time again. You can never truly say "You're over it" because the theme is changed five times a year. This includes Winter, Chinese New Year, Spring, Summer, and last but not least Fall. Pause, take a deep breath, be amazed by the celestial scents of these Real flowers, some replaced every two weeks.

Photo by George Landis

Flamingo Wildlife Habitat

Take a trip to this mini Zoo, for Free! It's nice to let your kids run around a bit and get some fresh air. Set your sites on these fancy pink Flamingos, koi fish, turtles, and pelicans.

THE "BUGSY BUILDING"

ON THIS SITE, BENJAMIN "BUGSY" SIEGEL'S ORIGINAL
FLAMINGO HOTEL STOOD FROM DECEMBER 26, 1946
UNTIL DECEMBER 14, 1993.

THE HOTEL, WHICH HOUSED 77 ROOMS, INCLUDING
THE NOTORIOUS MR. SIEGEL'S "BUGSY SUITE,"
OR "PRESIDENTIAL SUITE," AS IT WAS SOMETIMES
REFERRED TO, WAS UNIQUE IN MORE WAYS
THAN ONE. THE WINDOWPANES, FOR INSTANCE,
WERE BULLET-PROOF, AND, ALTHOUGH THERE
WAS ONLY ONE ENTRANCE TO THE TOP-FLOOR
SUITE, THERE WERE FIVE POSSIBLE EXITS. THIS
INCLUDED A HIDDEN LADDER LEADING FROM
THE HALLWAY CLOSET TO A BASEMENT TUNNEL,
WHICH LED TO AN UNDERGROUND GARAGE,
WHERE BUGSY ALLEGEDLY HAD A CHAUFFEURED
GETAWAY CAR AWAITING AT ALL TIMES.

BUT MR. SIEGEL'S PREOCCUPATION WITH SAFETY
AND ESCAPE ROUTES PROVED TO BE GEOGRAPHICALLY
MISPLACED. ON JUNE 20, 1947, 300 MILES FROM
LAS VEGAS, AT THE BEVERLY HILLS MANSION
OF HIS GIRLFRIEND, VIRGINIA HILL, BUGSY
WAS KILLED IN A HAIL OF GUNFIRE BY UNKNOWN
ASSAILANTS.

SINCE THAT DAY, THE FLAMINGO HAS CHANGED
OWNERSHIP 4 TIMES, INCLUDING ITS FINAL SALE
FROM PARK PLACE ENTERTAINMENT IN 2005.

BENJAMIN "BUGSY" SIEGEL

Bugsy Siegel's Memorial

A moment of silence as we pay our respects to the Entrepreneurial Legend Mobster, Mr. Benjamin "Bugsy" Siegel. He had a vision of what Las Vegas could and would become, sadly Mr. Siegel's life was taken way too early. But while he was here, rest assured he made a Great name for himself.

Town Square Children's Park

6605 Las Vegas Blvd South. It's a Park, let your kids safely run Wild!

Photo by George Landis

Bellagio's Fountain Show

This Water Show is spectacular and breathtakingly free. Don't sweat it if you miss the show, lucky for you and the family, it repeats every 30 minutes starting at Noon weekends and 3pm weekdays and every 15 minutes from 7pm. To midnight. Unknown fact, That water is the water you just showered with, HIGH FIVE Las Vegas for recycling and being drought conscious!

Free Circus Acts at Circus Circus

Don't miss these Carnival Midway Giveaways brought to you by Circus Circus, showtimes starting at 1:30pm Monday – Thursday and 11:30 am Friday – Sunday.

Glitter Gulch aka Fremont Street

Experience this at least once, it can get a little overwhelming with the kids and all, but if you go right before the sun goes down you'll miss the daytime crowd and you can leave right before "The Freaks come out at night."

Hotel/Resort Exploring

When all else fails, throw the itinerary out the window and just get Lost in VEGAS! There's amazement around every corner no matter which Hotel you're in, I promise!

Photo by George Landis

The Volcanos at The Mirage

Like Siblings, we feel that the Bellagio fountain show and the Mirage Volcano show go hand and hand. Time them correctly to catch both shows; and the family is in for a good time, at no cost to Mom and Dad. This Volcano erupts daily, every hour from 8-11pm.

Aria Express Free Tram Ride on the Strip

Give everyone's feet a rest on Aria's Express Tram Ride. This tram runs from Park MGM through Aria, and back on to the Bellagio so you can see that Fountain Show.

Photo by George Landis

"Welcome to Fabulous Las Vegas" Sign

Going strong since 1959. All Families must take up this Iconic photo opportunity at some point or another. It's pretty much the Las Vegas Strip right of passage!

6

"Viva Las Vegas" Top 10 Family Friendly Eats

A long with being known as the Entertainment Capital of the World, Las Vegas is also known as the Overpriced Food Capital of the World. Here are 10 places the Family can enjoy and still have money left over for the rest of the vacation.

<u>ON the Strip</u>
    Shake Shack $$
    Mr. Mamas Breakfast & Lunch $
    Carmine's Italian Restaurant (Huge portions, Share!) $$
    Village Street Eateries New York New York $$-$$$
    In n Out Burger $

OFF The Strip

Egg Works $$

Tacos El Gordo $

The Modern Vegan $$

Maryland Crab Corner $$

John Incredible Pizza Co. (FUN ALERT!) $$

7

"Meanwhile in Vegas..." Best Pools for Kids

Mandalay Bay Resort

Stepping out into the pool area is like you've somehow teleported to the Beach. It's pretty insane, from the sandy white beach area to the Ginormous Wave Pool, not to mention you have your choice of 3 Huge Pools, you will be in BEACH PARADISE. If you just feel like floating and getting lost into sweet nothingness jump into the Lazy River and float away. This Pool is free for hotel guests, daily pool passes available for purchase.

The Tank at the Golden Nugget

Swim alongside the sharks in "The Tank" at the Golden Nugget. This pool is AWESOME JAWS! (Sorry, I had to throw at least one corny Mom joke in this book, congrats you found it!) For an extra fee, you can take a ride through the Shark tank via slide, or be a guest for one of the Golden Nugget's Shark Tank Tour Shows. The Tank is free for hotel guests, daily pool passes available for purchase.

The Grand Pool at MGM

Can you say, Labyrinth of pools? That is what MGM has in store for you with 6.5 acres of Pool time fun. Lounge chairs are first come first serve, and tube rentals available purchase. The Grand Pool is free for hotel guests, daily pool passes available for purchase. Come early so you don't end up on the waitlist.

The Beach Club Pool at Flamingo Hotel

The Tropical scene surrounding the Flamingo's 4 pools is enough to get my family there. The main pool is also a central point to a Lagoon, a Waterfall, and a Water Slide. The Beach Club Pool is free for hotel guests, daily pool passes available for purchase. Let's go kids, the Flamingo pool awaits.

The Splash Zone at Circus Circus

Circus Circus' Pool area is fun for kids of ALL ages, they have a "Splash Zone '' which is like a mini water park, a pool and a HUGE 3 person, 50 ft TALL Water Slide. The Splash Zone Pool is free for hotel guests, daily pool passes available for purchase.

Cancun Resort

Offers a Massive Pool area that does not disappoint with waterfalls, FOUR different water slides, and a hidden Jacuzzi. Oh yea, i'm sure that sounds nice for all the parents who are sore from all the Vegas strip walking.

Garden of the Gods Pool Oasis at Caesars Palace

This Roman themed pool paradise is so amazing that it is "exclusively" for Caeser's Palace and Nobu Hotel guests only. My family and I have gotten in and enjoyed this pool and its amenities very discreetly, because sharing is caring! It's refreshing, and stunning with all its Roman Empire Statues. Thank you Caesar, it's been great hanging with you, gotta go!

8

"Vegas NATURE State of Mind" The other Part of Las Vegas

Red Rock Canyon

25 Miles West of Las Vegas Strip.

There are over 100 Trails available to the public here at Red Rock

Canyon. I'm sure you're thinking "Wow, what a great help!" Mom to mom, I wish I had known this about our now favorite trail, before our first visit. Lost Canyon Trail is the trail for my readers. I know how hard it can be traveling with kids, so this trail is perfect for just that. Try to visit during the spring season to get a peak at the rarest of rares, a Waterfall in the Desert. Pack sunscreen, power snacks, and lots of water to fight off that desert heat and dehydration.

Gilcrease Orchard

20 Miles North of Las Vegas Strip

This Family owned Orchard is a great place to take the kids, a day on the farm is exactly what's needed after all that arcade gaming and candy eating. Plan your trip to Gilcrease early fall so you can pick your own sunflowers! They also have an awesome Pumpkin Patch if your family loves Halloween as much as mine.

Mount Charleston

43 Miles North of Las Vegas Strip, Some quiet time is just what is needed after a couple of days in Las Vegas. I personally have to become one with nature frequently or the crazy starts to show. Thank goodness for Mount Charleston, there are over 60 miles of trails here to accommodate your level of Hike activities. All families are different and we all can enjoy these hikes at our own pace. Don't forget snacks, water, and sunscreen.

Spring Preserve

6 Miles North of Las Vegas Strip

This Spring Preserve may look serene and peaceful in all its photographed beauty, but it actually gets pretty lively once all the tourists flood in. Being the closest option to the Strip is what makes this one the Winner. They have so many fun-filled activities to keep our kids busy while you enjoy the fresh air.

Nelson's Landing, Cliff Jumping

45 Miles South/East of Las Vegas Strip

Beat the Las Vegas heat by jumping off a Cliff! Yea, you heard me right, If everyone jumps off this cliff you bet your tush doing it too. Nelson's Landing has cliffs ranging 10-30 ft, please use your best judgment and be safe. If there are Locals around, ask for cliff jumping advice first. You can also just get in the water like a normal person, no judgment.

Emerald Cove

57 Miles South of Las Vegas Strip. This is well worth driving an hour away for the day, the emerald colored water was not only admirable, but it felt so nice in the Nevada heat. We got to experience the Cove Cave, it's a spectacular site to see. When the sun hits just right, the whole inside of the cave lights up in different colors of blues mixed with greens. Don't shortchange your family by giving the excuse that "it's too far to drive!" Live in the present as tomorrow is not promised. Mom tip, please make sure to pack sunscreen, water and snacks, or even a whole picnic set up if possible. Water adventures can make us super hungry. We searched for a deal online to rent a few family kayaks and made a fun-filled outdoors day out of this. You will not regret this choice.

9

"That's all Folks!" Leaving Las Vegas

Conclusion

I hope you have enjoyed reading this Las Vegas Travel Guide "Family Edition" as much as I did writing it. We live, eat, breathe, all for our kids; don't let a moment go by that you are not in awe of the Family surrounding you. I made this guide to help all Parents alike be able to take their families of 3,4,5, even 6 like me. On their very own Las Vegas Adventure, and not be burdened by the millions, sometimes overwhelming choices of places to go, sites to see, pools to swim, and things to eat. CHEERS! Stay safe, and go out there and make as many fun everlasting sweet memories as possible.

If I have steered you and your family successfully through the streets of Las Vegas, Please be sure to leave me a review letting me know. I would love to hear about your family's trip. What was your favorite part about this guide, and what you were excited to try with the fam. If you'd really like to make my day show at least one pic from the photo challenge! C'mon, let's see the "Welcome to Las Vegas Family pic." Thank you to the parents who purchased this book. It's the best feeling in the world knowing you've made someone else's life a bit easier.

-Jen

10

Resources

Love Exploring. (2020, September 2). *Sin City secrets: the incredible story of Las Vegas.* Loveexploring.Com. Retrieved 30 August 2022, from https://www.loveexploring.com/gallerylist/99342/sin-city-secrets-the-incredible-story-of-las-vegas

Wulff, A. (2017, January 14). *A Brief History of Las Vegas as We Know It Today.* Culture Trip. Retrieved 30 August 2022, from https://theculturetrip.com/north-america/usa/nevada/articles/a-brief-history-of-las-vegas-as-we-know-it-today/

Las Vegas Kids. (2022, March 2). *25 Best Vegas Hotels for Kids and Family.* Retrieved 30 August 2022, from https://www.lasvegaskids.net/hotels/las-vegas-hotels-landing/

Las Vegas Kids. (n.d.). *7 Affordable & Amazing Family-Friendly Eats Just Off the Strip.* 7 Affordable & Amazing Family-Friendly Eats Just Off the Strip. Retrieved 30 August 2022, from https://www.lasvegaskids.net/dining/7-affordable-amazing-family-friendly-eats-just-off-the-strip/

Visit Las Vegas. (2022, June 14). *18 Things to Do in Las Vegas with Kids*. Family-Friendly Shows & Attractions. Retrieved 30 August 2022, from https://www.visitlasvegas.com/experience/post/things-to-do-in-las -vegas-with-kids/

Vegas Family Guide. (2021, June 22). *Top 5 Kids Hikes in Red Rock Canyon*. Retrieved 30 August 2022, from https://vegasfamilyevents.com/top-5- red-rock-kids-hikes/

Mowat, L. (2022, August 24). *Spring Mountains Weekly Update*. Go Mt. Charleston. Retrieved 30 August 2022, from https://www.gomtcharlest on.com/

Mullennix, B. (2022, May 8). *Nelson's Landing Cliff Jumping (Las Vegas Day Trip!)*. Feeling Vegas. Retrieved 30 August 2022, from https://www.f eelingvegas.com/nelsons-landing-cliff-jumping/

Printed in Great Britain
by Amazon

18646719R00051